Rarities
in
Carnival Glass

by

Bill Edwards

COLLECTOR BOOKS
A Division of Schroeder Publishing Co., Inc.

Additional copies of this book may be ordered from:

COLLECTOR BOOKS
P. O. Box 3009
Paducah, Kentucky 42001

@ $8.95

Copyright: Bill Edwards, Bill Schroeder, 1978
ISBN 0-89145-075-0

This book or any part thereof may not be reproduced without the written consent of the author and publisher.

DEDICATION

For Dave Kinney, who is a real rarity - a true friend for the past twenty years.
And for my brother, Milford R. Edwards.

INTRODUCTION

RARITIES IN CARNIVAL GLASS

The dictionary defines the term "rare" as: highly esteemed because of uncommonness, valuable, or choice.

This definition applies to carnival glass also and it is our purpose in this book to show some of these choice, valuable or simply uncommon carnival glass items, many never pictured in a book before.

Many of the pieces of beautiful iridescent glass shown here are one-of-a-kind items that have sold for literally thousands of dollars each.

Others, while scarce and uncommon, are not favorites with collectors, despite their limited numbers. These pieces sell for very modest prices when they come on the market.

So, regardless of whether you have thousands to invest or simply several dollars now and then, there is something here for you - something that is a *rarity* in carnival glass.

ACKNOWLEDGEMENTS

Again, I wish to thank all those who offered their beautiful glass for me to use in this book:

        The Harold Ludemans
        The Carlton Schleedes
        Norma Morrison
        The Robert McCaslins
        Mary Estell
        Donald E. Moore
        The William Justices
        The Terry Henrys
        Don Doyle
        The Jack Wilsons
        The George Loeschers
        Robert Comer
        Lee Markley
        The Kenneth Abendroths
        Forrest Horr
        Linda Ledbetter
        Carol Moore
        The Robert Vinings

I never cease to be amazed at their warmth and generosity, and I cherish their friendship as much as their glass.

And, of course, a special thanks to my typist, Doris Kabel.

CONTENTS

Acorn Burrs Vase	9
Big Thistle Punch Bowl	10
Blackberry Wreath Plate, Millersburg	11
Bo Peep Mug & Plate	12
Butterfly and Corn Vase	13
Buzz Saw Cruet	14
Cambridge Cracker Jar	15
Chatelaine Pitcher	16
Checkerboard Water Set	17
Cherry Plate, Millersburg	18
Cherry/Hobnail Bowl, Millersburg	19
Cherry Powder Jar, Millersburg	20
Cherry Compote, Millersburg	21
Corn Bottle	22
Corn Vase - (Peach Opal)	23
Daisy Squares Goblet	24
Dance of the Veils Vase	34
Diamond and Sunburst Cruet	25
Diamond Points Basket	26
Dragon and Lotus (Aqua Opal)	27
Elks Paperweights	28
Emu Bowl	29
Estate Mug	30
Farmyard Plate	31
Feathered Serpent Spittoon	32
Fleur de Lis Rose Bowl	33
Fleur-de-Lis Vase	34
Floral and Optic Bowl (Red)	35
Flute Vase, Millersburg	36
Formal Hatpin Holder	37
Grape Goblet, Imperial	38
Grape, Water Bottle, Imperial	39
Grape Candlelamp, Northwood	40
Grape Centerpiece Bowl, Northwood	41
Grape Covered Compote & Card Tray, Northwood	42
Grape Cracker Jar, Northwood (Aqua Opal)	43
Grape Fernery, Northwood	44
Grape Stippled Humidor, Northwood (Blue)	45

Grape Master Punch Bowl, Northwood (Ice Blue)	
Grape Orange Bowl - Blackberry Interior, Northwood	
Grape Punch Set, Northwood (White)	
Grape Spittoon, Northwood	
Grape Sweetmeat, Northwood (Marigold)	
Harvest Bowl, Goddess of	
Heavy Hobnail Whimsey	
Hobnail Jardeniere, Millersburg	5_
Hobnail Pitcher	54
Hobstar and Feather Rosebowl	55
Hobstar and Feather Vase	56
Holly Sprig Sauce, Millersburg	57
Imperial Paperweight	58
Inca Vase	59
Inverted Feather Compote	60
Inverted Feather Punch Set	61
Inverted Strawberry Console Set	62
Jelly Jar	63
Little Barrels	64
Many Stars Bowl	65
Milady Waterset	66
Multi-Fruits and Flowers Pitcher, Millersburg	67
Multi-Fruits and Flowers Punch Set	68
Olympic Compote, Millersburg	69
Optic and Buttons Pitcher	70
Orange Tree Compote	71
Panelled Holly Pitcher	72
Peacock Plates, Millersburg	73
Peacock Ice Cream Bowl, Millersburg (Green)	74
Peacock "Proof", Millersburg (Marigold)	75
Peacock and Dalhia	76
Peacock and Urn Whimsey "Proof"	77
Peacock at the Fountain Orange Bowl (Aqua Opal)	78
Penny Match Holder	79
Persian Garden Chop Plate	80
Peter Rabbit Plate (Green)	81
Pinwheel Vases	82
Pipe Humidor (Green)	83
Primrose Bowl (Blue)	84
Rosalind Compote, Millersburg	85
Rose Column Experimental Vase	86
Rose and Greek Key Plate	87

uffled Rib Spittoon	88
ailboats Bowl	89
Sea Gulls Bowl	90
Sea Gulls Vase	59
Star Spray Brides Basket	91
Stippled Strawberry Spittoon	92
Swirl Mug	93
Taffeta Lustre Candlesticks	94
Town Pump (Marigold)	95
Tree Trunk Whimsey Jardeniere	96
Tropicana Vase	34
Vintage Bowls, Millersburg	97
Wheat Sweetmeat	98
Whirling Hobstar Punch Set (Unlisted)	99
Wildflower Compotes, Millersburg	100
Wild Rose Syrup	101
Wild Rose Bowl (Ice Blue)	102
Zipper Loop Lamps	103

ACORN BURRS VASE

$1000.00

Here is a very unique rarity that I'm very pleased to show, for none other has been reported or shown in any carnival glass book before now.

It is a whimsey, shaped from a tumbler and the color rivals any piece of carnival glass I've seen. A truly rare and beautiful gem.

BIG THISTLE PUNCH BOWL

Bowl and Base
$5800.00

    I could spend pages raving about this very superb rarity, but let me simply say I consider it the most beautiful of *all* the carnival glass punch bowls.

    Two are known and both are amethyst. One has a flared top while the other is straight up.

    Needless to say, the glass is clear, the mold work superior and the iridescence beyond belief.

MILLERSBURG BLACKBERRY WREATH PLATE

$395.00

Though the piece pictured is not rare, the pattern is one to remember. Pictured is the Blackberry Wreath bowl. The Blackberry Wreath plate, 6" in amethyst has appeared only once and I know of one chop plate and 5 small ones in marigold.

These have all been shaped from the bowl pattern and why more weren't turned out is a mystery. They are truly a beautiful example of the glassmakers art.

BO PEEP MUG AND PLATE

Plate - $200.00   Mug - $95.00

While the Bo Peep mug is simply scarce, the plate is a quite rare item, seldom sold or traded from one collection to another. The color is good marigold and reminds us of that found on most of the Fenton Kitten items.

Of course, all children's items in glass were subjected to great loss through breakage, but I doubt if large amounts of the Bo Peep pattern were made to begin with; so of course small quantities have survived. It is presumed to be a Fenton product.

BUTTERFLY AND CORN VASE

$750.00

    This interesting vase is rare for several reasons and it is a pleasure to show it here.

    First is the pattern which has been reported only twice in the past few years. Both examples are identical in size (5 7/8" tall and 2 3/4" base diameter).

    Secondly, the base color of the glass is vaseline with a marigold finish.

    While this coloring is found rarely on both Millersburg and Northwood items, I believe the Butterfly and Corn vase to be a product of the latter.

BUZZ SAW CRUET

No stopper - $200.00   Complete - $325.00

This eagerly hunted Cambridge novelty always brings top dollar when it comes up for sale.

Found in two sizes, the colors seen are green or marigold. The mold-work is fantastic as is the iridescence.

Oddly, the base shows a pontil mark indicating the cruet was blown into a mold.

Normally, the Buzz Saw Cruet, was sold with a matching glass stopper, but the one shown (like so many around today) has long since lost the stopper.

Again, these were probably designed as containers for some liquid, but just what, we can't say.

CAMBRIDGE CRACKER JAR
(UNLISTED)

$500.00

Here is a carnival glass rarity I didn't know existed until I was fortunate enough to get this photo of it.

The lid is missing on this one and I haven't any idea what name it should be called, but it certainly is a beautiful thing. The mold-work ranks with the best from the Cambridge Company and the color reminds us of the Buzz Saw cruet.

CHATELAINE PITCHER

$2000.00

    Here is a pitcher, attributed by many to the Imperial Glass Company, that seldom trades owners and always high-lights any collection.
    Not only is it rare and beautiful, but the workmanship is top quality all the way.

CHECKERBOARD WATER SET

Tumbler - $300.00 ea. Pitcher - $3000.00

It has been pretty well established that the Checkerboard Water Set was a Westmoreland product, which partially explains its rarity today.

I've seen about half a dozen tumblers over the years but the pitcher shown is one of only three known to exist.

The color, iridescence and mold-work are outstanding.

MILLERSBURG CHERRY PLATES

6" Plate - $285.00   Chop Plate - $900.00

Here is another chance to show two rare sizes of a Millersburg plate shape.
The 6" marigold is one of three known and the green cherry chop plate is the only reported example in this color and size.
Simply spectacular! Items like these are what make Millersburg a magic name.

MILLERSBURG CHERRY/ HOBNAIL BOWL

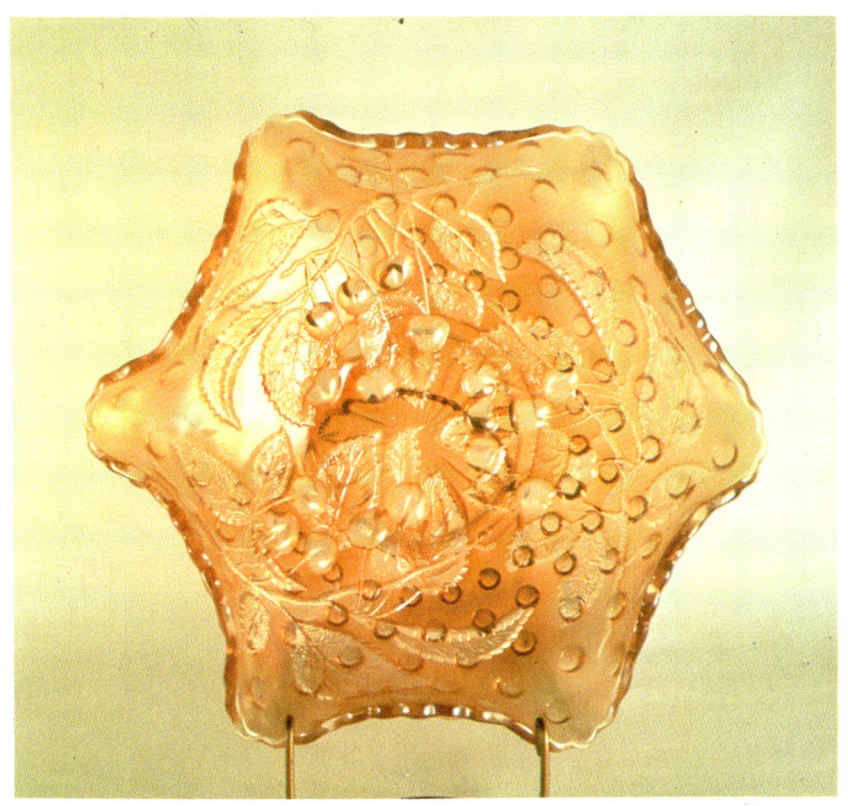

$600.00

Please stop and compare this to the Vintage bowls with hobnail exteriors shown elsewhere in this book. Then, realizing how rare *they* are, just imagine how very important the Millersburg Cherry bowl with hobnail exterior is. Besides the marigold one shown, amethyst does exist, but these are even rarer than the Vintage bowls!

MILLERSBURG CHERRY POWDER JAR

$450.00

Most collectors, even those who are Millersburg "addicts" do not realize this little beauty exists for I've heard of only three examples (two owned by one lucky family!)

The coloring is green, typical of a Millersburg product, with super iridescence.

The size is 3½" tall and 3¾" wide.

MILLERSBURG CHERRY COMPOTE

$500.00

Again we show a fantastic Millersburg rarity as are most compotes from that Company.

While more amethyst Cherry compotes are known than green or marigold, *any* color in this shape is highly desirable and brings top dollar whenever one is sold.

Roughly 6½" tall by 7¼" across the bowl, the Cherry compote has the same stem and base shape as the Millersburg Poppy compote.

The interior is plain and both the inside and outside are highly iridized. The mold work is outstanding.

CORN BOTTLE

$225.00

While I can't be certain, I've always felt this cute little rarity was an Imperial Glass product. But regardless of the manufacturer, it is a beautifully molded, highly lustered novelty item found in smoke, green, amethyst and marigold.

Standing only 4¼" tall, the Corn Bottle usually is found with a cork stopper and I feel certain no other lid ever existed.

It has been suggested possible uses might have been a syrup holder, a sugar shaker or even a whiskey sample bottle! Take your choice for all are plausible.

CORN VASE - (PEACH OPAL)

$395.00

    While it really does not show up well in the photo, this Northwood corn vase has a slight opalescence along the upper edge and is one of three classified as peach opalescent I've heard about.
    The marigold coloring on the rest of the vase is rich and even. All in all, this is a popular and rare piece of carnival glass.

DAISY SQUARES GOBLET

$385.00

    I showed two examples of the Daisy Squares rosebowl in my Millersburg book and they were quite rare; however, this goblet shape in a rich *amber* is much rarer and quite unusual.
    Millersburg pastel colors are just not often heard of and the few that do exist are quite spectacular.

DIAMOND AND SUNBURST CRUET

$1000.00

    I'm not in the least certain who made this very rare, very beautiful oil cruet, but I'm quite sure it would please any collector of beautiful glass.
    The color is green with much yellow in the mix causing an amberish appearance.
    It measures 2¼" across the base and stands 7" tall with the ribbed stopper in place.
    The iridescence is rather light and watery.

DIAMOND POINTS BASKET

$350.00

    Although the dimensions are nearly the same as Northwood's Basket, the Diamond Points Basket is a much rarer pattern.
    And while some collectors have credited the Fenton Company with this much sought novelty, I lean toward Northwood as the maker.
    The colors found are marigold, purple and a radiant cobalt blue. The mold work is sharp and precise and the iridescence heavy and outstanding. I have heard of less than a dozen of these baskets, so lucky are you if you own one.

DRAGON AND LOTUS (AQUA OPAL)

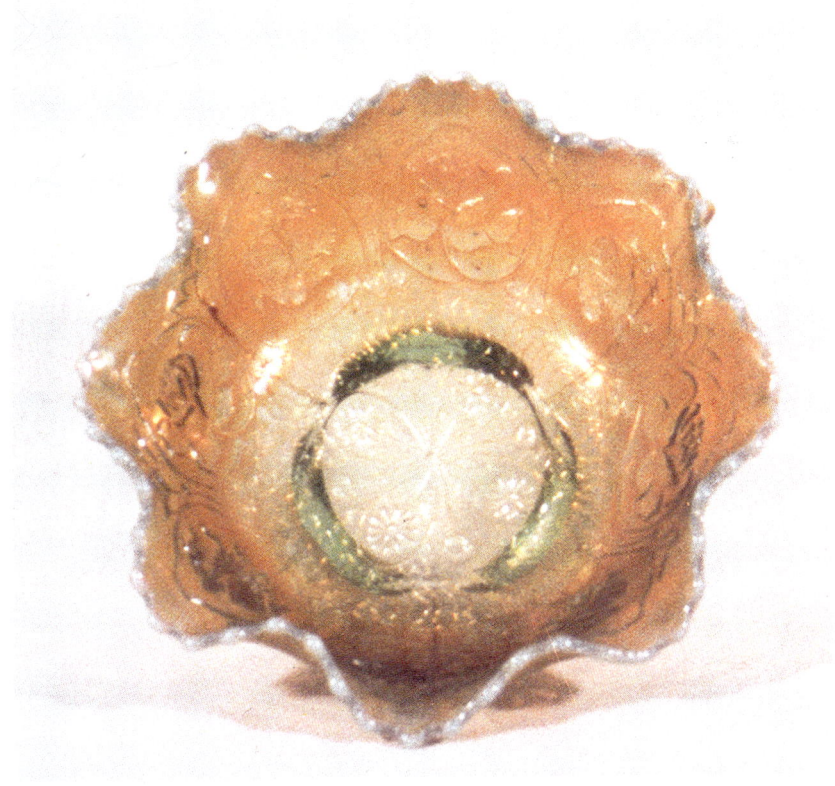

$200.00

Dragon and Lotus is, of course, a Fenton pattern and is quite available on marigold, cobalt and amethyst.

However it is only occasionally found on red base glass and even less often on the beautiful aqua color shown.

The spatula footed bowl is 8" wide, fluted and ruffled, with a plain exterior.

ELKS PAPERWEIGHTS

Purple - $800.00   Green - $1000.00

Once again we turn to a Millersburg rarity, but in this case actually double rarities for here are the amethyst and *green* Elks Paperweights.

To date only two green examples are known. Of course, both these beauties bring top dollar whenever they reach the marketplace and certainly deserve to.

EMU BOWL

$225.00

While I may be criticized for showing a piece of Australian carnival glass, the large Emu bowl is definitely rare enough to be included in a book of rarities, especially in the aqua coloring.

Known to be produced by the Crystal Glass Works of Sidney, every piece of Australian carnival glass is a quality product. Purple is the most often found color with marigold a distant second. I've seen no other patterns in the aqua base glass which has an amber lustre.

The Emu bowl measures 10¼" in width and is 4" deep.

ESTATE MUG

$75.00

    This rare little mug appears to belong in the late carnival era, but nevertheless is a much-in-demand item, especially to mug collectors.
    Most of these mugs are souvenir items and the one shown is no exception; it bears the inscription: "Souvenir of Gant, New York".
    The coloring is a pale marigold and the iridescence is only so-so. It measures 3" tall and heretofore is not listed in the major price guides.

FARM YARD PLATE

$8000.00

Spectacular is the only word to describe this unique rarity, the *only known plate* in this very beautiful Northwood pattern.

Notice how the shape allows the pattern to be viewed at its very best and of course the color is unbelievably rich.

The Farmyard plate is truly a masterwork of the glassmaker's art.

FEATHERED SERPENT SPITTOON

$2500.00

    Again I'm privileged to show a rare one-of-a-kind spittoon, turned from a small bowl by some inventive glass worker.
    I would certainly class the Feathered Serpent spittoon along with the Country Kitchen, the Nesting Swan and the Millersburg Peacock spittoons at the very summit of desirability and they surely must command enormous prices whenever they come up for sale.

FLEUR DE LIS ROSE BOWL

$500.00

    The Millersburg rarity shown is the collar base rose bowl and was, of course, shaped from the flat 8½" bowl. It is the only example reported.
    However, a sister rosebowl, also in sparkling amethyst glass, exists on a dome base.
    Needless to say, these exceptional whimsical items are rare jewels in carnival glass.

FLEUR-DE-LIS VASE
DANCE OF THE VEILS VASE
TROPICANA VASE

Fleur-de-Lis-$175.00   Dance of the Veils-$1500.00   Tropicana-$250.00

Although the vases on the left and right are not considered as rare as the Dance of the Veils vase in the center, they certainly aren't plentiful and it's a pleasure to show all three of them here.

The Fleur-de-lis vase was made by the Jenkins Company and is 10½" tall. It is heavy and deeply "intaglio" or cut in.

The Tropicana vase is 9" tall and its maker is unknown.

The Dance of the Veils vase is a Fenton product, 8 5/8" tall, and only a few are known by this author.

RED FLORAL AND OPTIC BOWL

$195.00

    While all examples of red iridized glass are rare, the larger items are more highly prized and some pieces have such outstanding coloring, they shine above the rest.

    Such an item is the Floral and Optic footed bowl shown. Made by the Imperial Glass Company, this pattern is quite common in marigold or clear carnival glass but the red is rare and desirable.

    It measures some 6" tall and is 8¼" in diameter. The interior is plain and does show some "stretch" effect around the outer edges.

MILLERSBURG FLUTE VASE

$400.00

While there may be some argument about this being called "Flute", it is certainly a Millersburg pattern.

Actually these are shaped from the large exterior bowl patterns used on the Strawberry bowls I show in my Millersburg book. Of course a plain plunger has been used to form the interior, but the base carries the identical star as the Strawberry bowl.

I know of two other examples of the Millersburg Flute vase; one is a vibrant green and the other is a very rare blue.

FORMAL HATPIN HOLDER

$150.00

While the Formal pattern has been attributed to the Imperial Glass Company, it has many features of products by the Northwood Company.

It is most often encountered as a bud vase or jack-in-the-pulpit vase, but rarely one finds a hatpin holder like the one shown. The color is normally a deep, deep purple with a sizeable amount of gold in the iridescence.

The Formal hatpin holder is 7¼" tall. Whenever one comes up for sale, it usually brings top dollar.

IMPERIAL GRAPE GOBLET

$65.00

    I suspect the reason so few of the old Grape Goblets were made by the Imperial Glass Company was because so much damage occurred when removing them from the mold since they are patterned completely inside and out.

    The colors are marigold, smoke, green, amber and purple and all are scarce and highly prized, especially the amber.

IMPERIAL GRAPE WATER BOTTLE

$250.00

While the Imperial Grape pattern was produced in large amounts in many shapes and is quite available today, there are a few shapes in this beautiful pattern which are rare. The water bottle is such a rarity.

The most often found color is the rich "helios" green Imperial was so famous for, but purple and marigold do exist. The rare clambroth color shown here is a true novelty and is the only example in this color I've run across.

The Imperial Grape water bottle is 8 ¾" tall and measures 5" across the widest area of the bottle. The lip is flared and *never* had a stopper.

NORTHWOOD GRAPE CANDLELAMP

$750.00

While the bases or candlesticks are only scarce, the complete lamp is quite rare, especially the marigold ones.

The height of the base is 5½" and the shades measure some 4". Thus, with the metal fitting necessary to join the two parts, the entire lamp is just under 11" in height.

Besides the marigold and purple, green ones are also known.

NORTHWOOD GRAPE CENTERPIECE BOWL

$450.00

The usual centerpiece bowl is turned in at the top like a rosebowl in this pattern and they are considered rare.

The example shown has been shaped into a very impressive item and is the only one I've seen with the flutes turned straight up.

The diameter of the bowl is 10½" and the coloring is very special.

NORTHWOOD GRAPE COVERED COMPOTE AND CARD TRAY

Compote - $2575.00   Card Tray - $150.00

Despite the fact that both of these rarities are Northwood Grape and both are scarcer in marigold than darker colors, the main reason for grouping them together is for a size comparison of the card tray, which is quite smaller than the less rare banana plate it resembles.

Of course the covered compote in marigold is also a highly prized, expensive rarity in its own right.

It stands 6½" tall and the bowl is 6½" in diameter.

NORTHWOOD GRAPE CRACKER JAR
(AQUA OPAL)

$1750.00

Once again we show a beautiful Northwood product in the rare and popular aqua opalescent finish.

This beauty measures 5 3/8" in diameter and 8" to the tip of the lid's finial.

I believe there are three or four of these reported so far and they rarely trade hands.

NORTHWOOD GRAPE FERNERY

Ice Blue - $3000.00

    The fernery is one Northwood Grape shape that is rare in any color, but is especially so in marigold, white, ice green and ice blue.
    Originally, it came with a glass or enameled liner and was actually used for small potted ferns or other green house-plants.
    It stands 4½" tall and is 7¾" wide.

NORTHWOOD GRAPE STIPPLED HUMIDOR (BLUE)

$2000.00

Certainly the Northwood Grape humidor is rare in any form, but the one shown, a *stippled* blue humidor is very rare. As in other shapes in this same pattern, very many more non-stippled examples seemed to have been produced.

At any rate, the Grape humidor is 7½" tall and has a diameter of 5½". Inside the lid is a three-finger sponge prong and the lid's finial has a leaf with grapes on top with beading on the edge.

NORTHWOOD GRAPE MASTER PUNCH BOWL (ICE BLUE)

$4000.00

    Shown is the only reported example of the Northwood Grape master or banquet size punch set in ice blue.
    It measures some 18½" tall by 17" across the fluted bowl and is extremely heavy glass. The color is sparkling and the iridescence is outstanding. All in all, a rare and impressive masterpiece of glass.

NORTHWOOD GRAPE ORANGE BOWL - BLACKBERRY INTERIOR

$1200.00

While this bowl is simply the well-known Northwood Grape orange bowl, it is the interior that makes it so unique. For as ⌐ around the inside of the bowl is a cable, grape leav⌐ *blackberries*.

I'm told only two of these impressive bowls ⌐ they are quite rare.

NORTHWOOD GRAPE PUNCH SET (WHITE)

$1200.00

The set shown is the 14" or "Medium size" Northwood Grape punch set and is extremely rare. Most of these sets found in frosty white are in the "?"-11" variety; however, there is one banquet or master set reported in color.

All in all, a very beautiful rarity with a delicate and subtle attraction all .

NORTHWOOD GRAPE SPITTOON

$5000.00 to $7000.00

Here are two of the three colors known in this very rare and coveted Northwood novelty; only the green is missing.

In size these measure only 2 5/8" tall and 3 1/8" across, but the prices are astronomical! A purple Grape spittoon sold in 1977 for $7,000.00!

We believe these were made from the sugar base molds as a rim is evident on most of them as if a lid had been planned.

NORTHWOOD SWEETMEAT (MARIGOLD)

$750.00

The sweetmeat is a shape peculiar in carnival glass only to the Northwood Company. This shape, a dainty deep, footed compote covered with a pagoda type top is found only on the Northwood Grape and Northwood Wheat patterns. In the former, while seen often on a purple base glass, it is seldom found on the marigold (green ones are found and are scarcer than the purple but less rare than marigold) base color.

GODDESS OF HARVEST BOWL

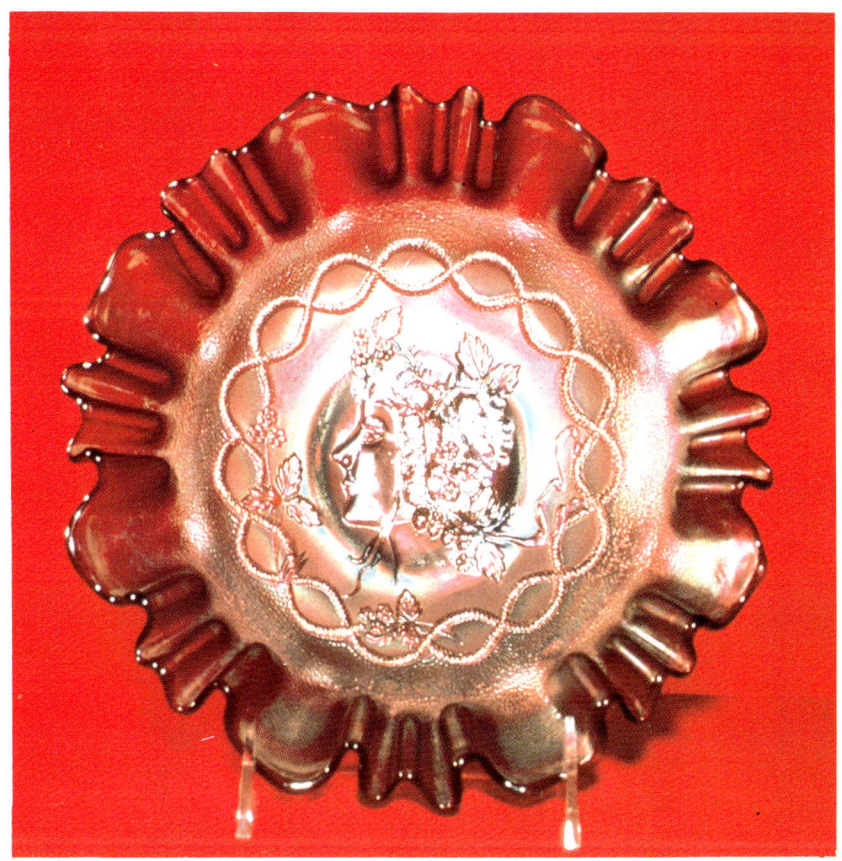

$3100.00

Make no mistake about this seldom-seen bowl. It is a rarity of the first order. As impressive in its own way as the Farmyard bowl, the Goddess of Harvest bowl was a Fenton product.

I've seen it in amethyst and blue but marigold has been reported.

Again, may I remind the reader just how few of these beauties are known to exist. I know of four- and how fortunate those lucky owners are. The going price now exceeds $3000.00 and they seldom are offered for sale.

HEAVY HOBNAIL WHIMSEY

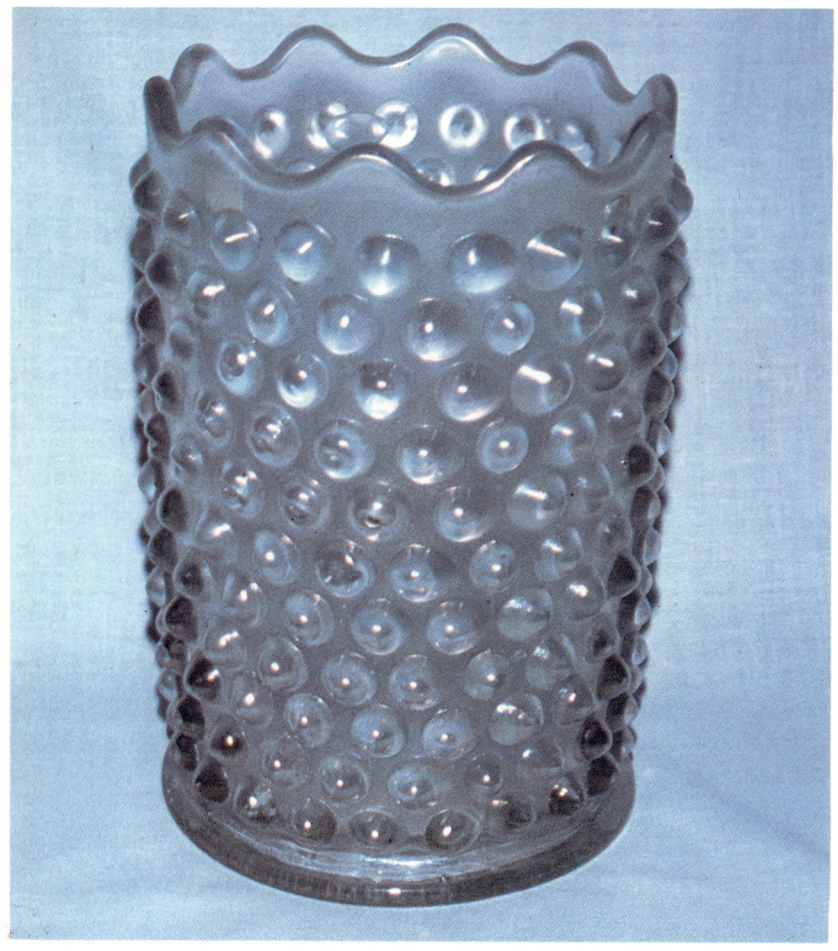

$175.00

    Perhaps this beauty was intended to be a vase; however, if so, its shape is quite unusual for one.
    It stands 7½" tall with a base diameter of 5½". The color is very frosty white with much gold in the irridescence. The base is plain, leading us to believe this was probably a product of the Fenton Glass Company, but that is pure speculation.
    Although I've seen smaller versions in white, this is the only reported example in this size.

MILLERSBURG HOBNAIL JARDENIERE

$575.00

Again, the Millersburg Company is credited with an extremely rare piece of carnival glass and certainly a beauty to behold.

While similar to their Hobnail Rosebowls and lady's spittoons, I really feel the Jardeniere is not from the same mold since there are more rows of hobnails and the size isn't the same.

I've heard of only this one example.

HOBNAIL PITCHER

$1800.00

    Let's have a closer look at this Millersburg product I showed in passing in my first book, for it rates a good deal of attention.
    Not only is it a rare pattern in water sets, but the mold work and color are outstanding. I know of about a dozen of these in colors of blue, amethyst and marigold and all are treasured highly.

HOBSTAR AND FEATHER ROSEBOWL

$950.00

Even though I showed this massive and impressive rosebowl in my Millersburg book, I had to show it in a solo performance because it is so rare and desirable (and because it is my favorite piece of carnival glass).

These rosebowls are found in green and purple and are about 9" tall. As you can see, the color is spectacular and the mold work ranks with the best.

HOBSTAR AND FEATHER VASE

$3800.00

While I showed this very rare Millersburg product in my first book, it was a green version while the one shown here is amythest.

Altogether there are four of these rarities reported, two in each color. They average about 16" tall and are very heavy with fine irridescence. They were pulled from the rosebowl in this pattern.

MILLERSBURG HOLLY SPRIG SAUCE

$175.00

Here is a cutie I fell in love with when I first saw it. It is from the Millersburg Company of course, so that had something to do with it, but just look at the *originality* in the design. The mold work is very superior and the color just great. I don't need to tell you how rare it is.

IMPERIAL PAPERWEIGHT

$750.00

    I had heard of this curious rarity but had not seen one until photographing it for this book.
    It is of solid, well iridized glass, 5½" long, 3¼" wide and 1¼" thick with a depressed center (probably for paper clips).
    Besides the three Imperial trademarks: NuArt, NuCut, and the Iron Cross mark, along one side is: IMPERIAL GLASS COMPANY BELLAIRE OHIO USA; and IMPERIAL ART GLASS on the other.
    All in all, a rare curiosity worthy of any collection.

INCA VASE
SEAGULLS VASE

Inca - $250.00   Seagulls - $250.00

Although the origin of these two vases is suspect - some think England -I wished to show them in this volume because they are both beautiful and unique.

I've never heard either pattern discussed in carnival circles and I doubt if many collectors know of their existence.

The coloring is rich and the mold work superior.

INVERTED FEATHER COMPOTE

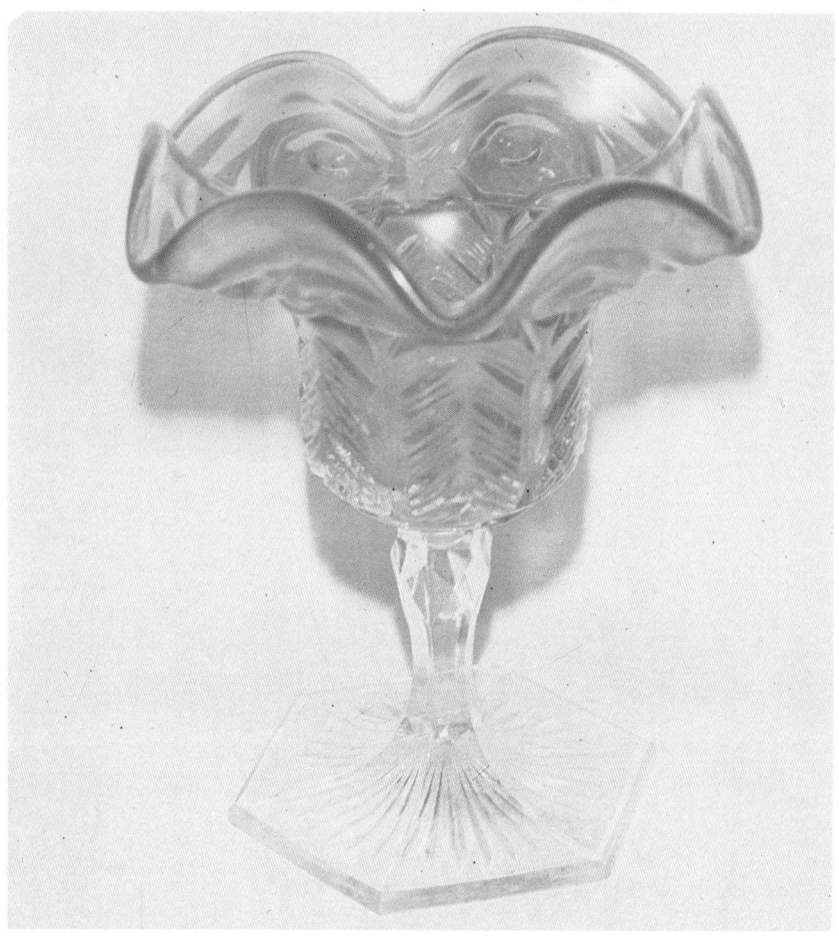

$40.00

Again we have a very scarce shape in the famous Cambridge Inverted Feather pattern and while more of these are available than the water set or the punch set in this pattern, the graceful little jelly compote is a real beauty.
I've seen about a dozen of these over the years and all of them were marigold with high iridescence on clear sparkling glass.

INVERTED FEATHER PUNCH SET

$1000.00

    The Cambridge Glass Company produced very small amounts of iridized glass and the Inverted Feather punch set is one of the very rare items.
    Besides this complete set in marigold, one other punch bowl and base in the same color is known, as well as a single cup and base in green.
    The glass is heavy and deeply impressed while the color is very rich like all of the Cambridge items I've seen.
    What a shame more of these aren't around!

INVERTED STRAWBERRY CONSOLE SET

Compote - $200.00   Candlesticks - $200.00 pair

Inverted Strawberry is a Cambridge pattern and is rare in all shapes and colors.

The candlesticks are highly sought and are seldom encountered with the centerpiece bowl shown, although they were designed as a 3-piece set.

Please note the lip of the compote which, unlike most, rolls out.

I've seen the candlesticks in marigold, amethyst and green while I haven't heard of a green centerpiece bowl to date.

The mold work is all intaglio or 'cut in" and is sharp and deep.

JELLY JAR

$50.00

    For years I found the lids to these Jelly Jars in shops and thought they were late carnival glass "coasters", but a few years back, I saw the two parts put together and was really quite surprised at what I saw.
    The jar itself is 3" wide and 2¾" tall and of deep, well iridized marigold. All the pattern is interior so that when the jar was upended onto the lid, a design was formed in the jelly.
    The lid itself also carries an interior design of spokes and an exterior one of a many rayed star.
    Again, here is a true rarity, well within any collector's range.

LITTLE BARRELS

$85.00 each

    Frankly, I'm not sure just what these little containers held-some say perfume or whiskey samples-but I do know they are well made, beautifully iridized little novelties.
    Only 3¾" tall, with a base diameter of 1 7/8", they are found in green, marigold, smoke and amber. The color is always super and the Little Barrell is a rare item, pretty enough to grace any collection.

MANY STARS BOWL

$165.00

    This beautiful Millersburg bowl is rare in the shape shown, the round (ice cream) bowl. Add to that its coloring, a light airy green just one step away from pastel green and you have a double rarity.
    The bowl measures just over 9" across and the finish is, of course, a beautiful radium gold luster.

MILADY WATERSET

Tumbler - $125.00   Pitcher - $795.00

This Fenton product is somewhat scarce in marigold or cobalt blue. However, in the beautiful *fiery* amethyst color shown, it is a very choice and rare item. The iridescence has much gold and adds greatly to the beauty. The tankard pitcher is 11½" tall and has a base diameter of 4¾".

MILLERSBURG MULTI-FRUITS AND FLOWERS PITCHERS

$5000.00 up - each

Please take a good close look at these two pitchers. The flat, slightly flared bottom is the one found on the one marigold, one green and two other known amethyst ones.

The other pitcher with a graceful tapering body must have been a pattern *sample* that was rejected because it is a loner. Notice how the shape resembles the Millersburg Cherry pitcher.

MULTI-FRUITS AND FLOWERS PUNCH SET

$750.00

Shown is the only known marigold Millersburg Multi-Fruits and Flowers punch set with a tulip-type top. Two green sets are known to exist and I suspect an amethyst will turn up eventually. At any rate, this is a favorite Millersburg pattern and much sought by collectors. The quality of glass and luster are exceptional.

MILLERSBURG OLYMPIC COMPOTE

$485.00

The Millersburg Olympic miniature compote is *extremely* rare and to date I've been privileged to see only this one. It's measurements are the same as the Leaf and Little Flowers compote made by the same company and the exterior and base are identical also.

If ever the old addage "Great things come in small packages" could apply, certainly it would be to the Olympic compote.

OPTIC AND BUTTONS PITCHER

$285.00

    I'm sure most collectors have seen this Imperial pattern on bowls, usually sizeable ones with two handles, but this quite rare pitcher has not been previously reported by any of the carnival glass pattern books.
    It is a beautiful deep marigold and has the old Imperial "iron cross" mark inside the base. It measures 8 5/8" across from the spout to the handle and stands 7" tall - a most unusual size for a pitcher and is quite similar to the Palm Beach pitcher in that respect.

ORANGE TREE COMPOTE

$45.00

While this miniature compote is not in itself rare, the number of green ones is very limited. In fact, very few shapes in the Orange Tree pattern in *green* are known.

The compote is slightly over 4" tall and measures only 3¾" across. The interior is plain and the stem is fluted.

The coloring is sensational with heavy iridescence both inside and out. The stem and base are not iridized.

PANELLED HOLLY PITCHER

$3000.00

    I am very happy to be able to show this very rare, one-of-a-kind water pitcher here. I had hoped to show it in my Northwood book, but got my signals crossed.

    At any rate, it is a very beautiful pitcher with outstanding color and workmanship.

MILLERSBURG PEACOCK PLATES

6" Plate - $250.00   Chop Plate - $1000.00

In order to show the size of the Millersburg Peacock chop plate, we've included one of the less rare 6" plates.

Actually either is a real find since only about a dozen of the smaller versions are known and 4 marigold chop plates are reported.

The finish is typically Millersburg with extra fine mold work.

MILLERSBURG PEACOCK ICE CREAM BOWL (GREEN)

$375.00

The Millersburg Peacock ice cream bowl is a rare bird in any color, but the beautiful green one shown is the rarest of all in this shape and pattern.
Without question it shows the design to perfection and the radium finish is fantastic while the glass is clear and sparkling.

MILLERSBURG PEACOCK "PROOF" - (MARIGOLD)

$200.00

If you are familiar with my book on Millersburg glass, you'll remember seeing this bowl shown in amethyst, of which five are known to exist.

Here, however, is the only reported marigold example of this super rarity and while I suspect others may exist, marigold in Millersburg is often ultra-rare.

PEACOCK AND DALHIA

$125.00

    Here is a cute little Fenton bowl not often found in any color, but in the cobalt blue shown is considered rare.
    It measures just 7" across and has the same odd exterior pattern as the Lion bowl - a panelled holly and leaf pattern on a stippled background.

PEACOCK AND URN WHIMSEY "PROOF"

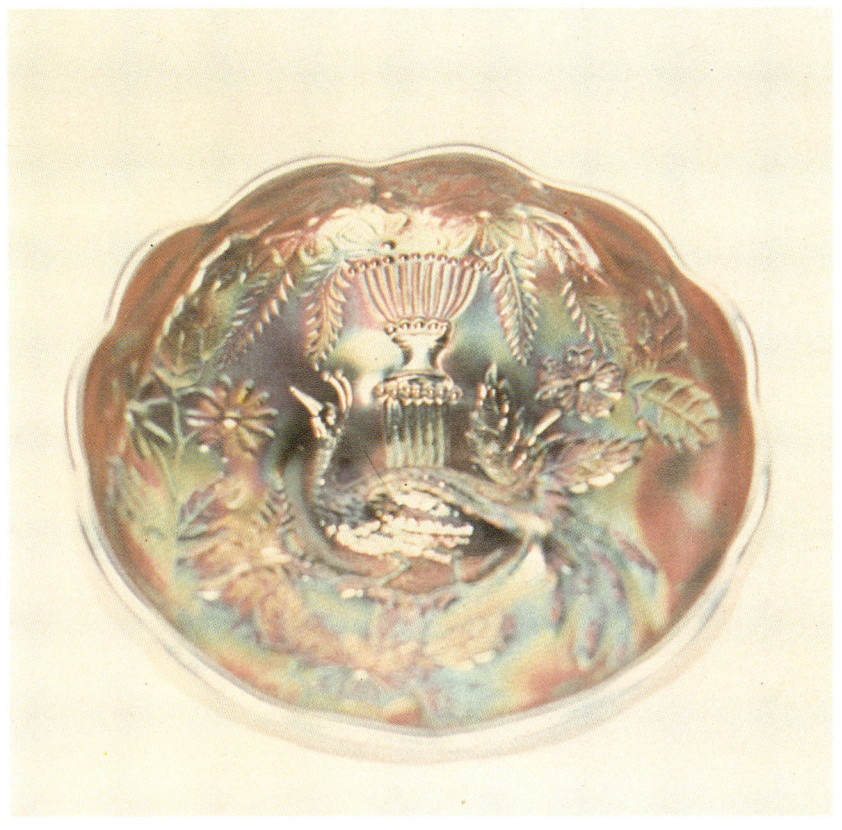

$100.00

At first glance, this appears to be an ordinary Northwood Peacock and Urn sauce bowl. However, on close examination, you can see there is *no bee* by the Peacock's beak!

This is the only example of this whimsey I've seen but like the Millersburg "proof" bowls, others probably exist.

PEACOCK AT THE FOUNTAIN ORANGE BOWL (AQUA OPAL)

$2800.00

The Peacock at the Fountain orange bowl is an impressive item in any color but in the very rare aqua opalescent, it becomes something to behold!

I've heard of three of these orange bowls and each and every one has brought an impressive price when put up for sale.

Of course this was one of Northwood's earlier iridized patterns and one of their best.

PENNY MATCH HOLDER

$85.00

Once again we picture a rare but useful novelty that is seldom found. The octagonal base is 3 3/8" across and the entire Match Holder is 3½" tall. Purple is the only color I've heard of and the iridescence is very rich and heavy, very much like the better Northwood products in this color, but the maker remains unknown.

PERSIAN GARDEN CHOP PLATE

$2000.00

Here is another very impressive rarity and the few I've seen have brought large amounts of money whenever sold.

Sometimes these 13" plates are referred to as sandwich trays but I prefer the chop plate description.

The color is very vibrant with much shimmering gold throughout.

PETER RABBIT PLATE (GREEN)

$1800.00

    The Peter Rabbit pattern is attributed to the Fenton Glass Company and is considered a top drawing card among the rarities in bowls. In plates, they are even more rare and show the pattern to superior advantage.
    The example shown is a superb green plate with rich golden luster. The mold work is superior to most I've seen.

PINWHEEL VASES

8" vase - $50.00   6½" vase - $85.00

    The smaller of these two vases was shown in my Millersburg book, but it wasn't until several months after its publication that the first (2 known) of the larger ones became known in carnival circles.

    There is some doubt as to their origin and some people feel they are English; however, they are rare in both sizes. The smaller version is 6½" tall while the larger measures 8" and has been reported in marigold only.

PIPE HUMIDOR (GREEN)

$2700.00

Here is another Millersburg pattern I showed in my first book in amethyst; however, the example above is a beautiful green with the watery gold radium finish the Millersburg Company was so famous for.

The mold work is especially good and of course the difficulty of producing this beauty without damage was extremely great.

BLUE PRIMROSE BOWL

$350.00

Shown is the only reported example of this choice Millersburg pattern in the very rare blue, a color seldom found in Millersburg items.

The iridescence is a brilliant *pink* and is like nothing else I've seen in carnival glass. The finish is satinized.

The blue Primrose bowl is a beautiful and unique rarity, a true gem in color, finish and mold work and would certainly be the crowning jewel in any collection.

MILLERSBURG ROSALIND COMPOTE

Master Compote - $400.00   Jelly Compote - $300.00

Here are two varieties of compotes most collectors hadn't heard of until quite recently and of course both are very rare.

The larger compote is about 8" tall. Two of these are known to exist in marigold.

The smaller compote, called a Jelly compote, has a different stem and base as you can see. Two amethyst ones are reported.

ROSE COLUMN EXPERIMENTAL VASE

$1000.00

Here is a variation of a rare vase that is even rarer still, for I know of no other like it.

Prior to firing, the alternating rows of roses have been colored red and gold while the leaves have been made green! The result is a unique and beautiful vase that would enhance any collection.

ROSE AND GREEK KEY PLATE

$1500.00

This very beautiful square plate is a sight to behold. Not only is it quite unique but so very well designed that I simply can not understand why there aren't more of these. But alas, there's only the one known.

The coloring is a smokey amber. The plate measures 8½" across and the roses are deep and hollow on the underside, much like the well-known Rose Show bowls.

RUFFLED RIB SPITTOON

$150.00

    This little cutie could be called Fine Rib or Lustre and Clear I guess but I feel the name given is more appropriate.
    At any rate the coloring is a good rich marigold and the ribbing is on the interior.
    The spittoon stands 4" tall and has a rim diameter of 4½" with a collar base diameter of nearly 2".
    I haven't a notion who the maker is, but the finish looks much like Imperial or Northwood.

SAILBOATS BOWL

$85.00

Most often encountered in marigold, this neat little sauce bowl is rare in red and even rarer in the green shown.
It is only 5½" across and is very shallow. The Sailboats pattern was made by the Fenton Art Glass Company.

SEA GULLS BOWL

$85.00

If one rarity in this book stands as an example of "scarce but not prized", the Sea Gulls bowl is that rarity.

Certainly there are far less of these to be found than many items that bring 10 times the money, but for some strange reason, these cuties are not sought by most collectors.

The two bird figures are heavily detailed as is the bowl pattern. The color, while not outstanding, is good and is iridized both inside and out.

The diameter of the bowl is 5 3/4" and the depth is 2 7/8". I believe the manufacturer was Jeanette but I could be wrong.

STAR SPRAY BRIDE'S BASKET

$100.00

Now and then this Imperial pattern is found in crystal or marigold carnival glass; however, the smoke color is quite scarce and this is the only example I ever found of the complete bride's basket.

The bowl measures 7½" in diameter and has a very beautiful finish. The metal holder is nicely done, having a fine gold overspray and tiny rosettes with leaves on the handle.

STIPPLED STRAWBERRY SPITTOON

$400.00

    While this pattern has been reported previously in a tumbler only, it obviously wasn't limited to that shape, and it is a real pleasure to show this rare spittoon shape.
    It stands 3½" tall and measures 4½" across its widest part.
    The coloring is nothing spectacular but adequate.
    Along the spittoon's lip is a checkerboard pattern. The manufacturer is unknown.

SWIRL MUG

$50.00

    While the Northwood Swirl pattern is difficult to find in its other limited shapes - namely, tumblers and pitchers (two varieties), it is the mug that is really scarce.
    In fact the one shown is only the second I've seen and it is not listed in the two major price guides.
    The color is excellent, being a rich deep marigold and the glass is clear and sparkling.
    The Swirl pattern is, of course, an interior one.

TAFFETA LUSTRE CANDLESTICKS

$250.00 pr.

These very rare Fostoria candlesticks were manufactured in 1916 or 1917 (according to an old Fostoria catalog) in colors of amber, blue, green, crystal or orchid. They were part of a "flower set" which included a center piece bowl 11" in diameter.

The candlesticks themselves came in 2, 4, 6, 9 and 12 inch sizes and as you can see, these still have the original paper labels on the bottom.

When held to the light, the ultra-violet color is fantastic and the iridescence is heavy and rich.

Fostoria made very small amounts of iridized glass and certainly these examples of their Taffeta Lustre line are quite rare.

TOWN PUMP (MARIGOLD)

$850.00

While this well-known Northwood pattern is considered rare in any color, the marigold is much rarer than purple.

The color is rich and vibrant with the pink and blue highlights only the Northwood Company seemed capable of managing in their marigold.

TREE TRUNK
WHIMSEY JARDENIERE

$200.00

    Most collectors of Carnival Glass are familiar with the well-known Northwood Tree Trunk vase, but here is one that was never pulled into the vase shape. If it had been completed, I'm sure it would have been close to two feet tall; however, it's present measurements are 9¾" tall and 10½" across the ruffled top.
    The color is a very beautiful purple with high luster.
    Truly an impressive and rare whimsey.

MILLERSBURG VINTAGE BOWLS

From $350.00 to $500.00

The four bowls shown pretty well cover the spectrum of this highly prized Millersburg pattern and include a green, blue and marigold bowl in the 9½" size as well as the super-rare green 5½" sauce. All of them carry the hobnail exterior the Millersburg Company was so famous for and each and every one is rare and much-sought item.

WHEAT SWEETMEAT

$2000.00

    I showed this very, very rare pattern in my Northwood book; however, it certainly rates a space among the rarities too.

    Besides the two known sweetmeats, there is one reported bowl in the wheat pattern.

    Needless to say, these sweetmeats sell for huge prices whenever they hit the market and are real "show stoppers".

WHIRLING HOBSTAR PUNCH SET (UNLISTED)

$85.00 Set

This quite unusual punch set is smaller than many others and the light even iridescence indicates it came along late in the carnival glass era; but it is certainly not new carnival glass and isn't listed in any of the guides as far as I know. I'd guess Jeanette made it or Imperial.
There are six cups.

MILLERSBURG WILDFLOWER COMPOTES

Jelly - $395.00   Reg. - $350.00

I showed the standard Wildflower compote in my Millersburg book, but here I'm privileged to show both that and the jelly compote so rarely seen.

I must admit I'm completely captured by compotes and these two really "turn me on". They certainly are beautiful.

WILD ROSE SYRUP

$525.00

Here is a strange rarity indeed, for as far as I can ascertain, it is the only iridized syrup known.

Seen only in marigold of rich color and adequate lustering, the Wild Rose Syrup is very attractive.

The maker is thus far unknown, but the mold work is quite similar to that of many of Harry Northwood's products.

Measuring 6½" tall, the syrup holds 12 fluid ounces and has a metal top.

WILD ROSE BOWL (ICE BLUE)

$275.00

Most every collector of carnival glass has seen this pattern, especially in green or marigold, but the one shown is the only ice blue example I've heard of.

And on close examination, you will note the exterior is different from the standard Wildrose pattern as are the feet.

This may have been a sample that was later modified for mass production.

OTHER BOOKS
FOR CARNIVAL GLASS COLLECTORS

Millersburg, Queen of Carnival Glass, 5½ x 8½, full color, current values
by Bill Edwards .... $ 8.95

Northwood, King of Carnival Glass, 5½ x 8½, full color, current values
by Bill Edwards .... $ 8.95

The Collector's Encyclopedia of Carnival Glass, 8½ x 11, hardbound, full color, current values
by Sherman Hand .... $ 19.95

Carnival Glass Price Guide, 7th Edition, 5½ x 8½, hundreds of current values, illustrated
by Sherman Hand .... $ 3.95

Ask for these books at your favorite bookstore or order direct.

COLLECTOR BOOKS
P.O. Box 3009
Paducah KY 42001

ZIPPER LOOP LAMPS

Marigold - $200.00   **Smoke - $250.00**

Shown are two of the three sizes in these kerosene lamps made by the Imperial Glass Company. Only the small hand lamp is missing. The colors are marigold of very good color, and the rare smoky carnival Imperial was so famous for.

While not as rare as the Millersburg Wild Rose lamp, these are nevertheless choice and would grace any collection.